The WEED was a FLOWER

The WEED was a FLOWER

Gary West

authorHOUSE®

AuthorHouse™
1663 Liberty Drive
Bloomington, IN 47403
www.authorhouse.com
Phone: 1-800-839-8640

Interior Graphics/Art Credit: Ralph West

Published by AuthorHouse   04/24/2012

ISBN: 978-1-4685-9561-1 (sc)
ISBN: 978-1-4685-9562-8 (e)

Any people depicted in stock imagery provided by Thinkstock are models, and such images are being used for illustrative purposes only.
Certain stock imagery © Thinkstock.

This book is printed on acid-free paper.

Because of the dynamic nature of the Internet, any web addresses or links contained in this book may have changed since publication and may no longer be valid. The views expressed in this work are solely those of the author and do not necessarily reflect the views of the publisher, and the publisher hereby disclaims any responsibility for them.

Contents

Norman, E. W.
And George Washington Carver
Edinburg's African-American Schools
1928-1961

The following is a brief history of the two schools which served the African-American children of Edinburg, Texas and some of the people associated with them.

Rev. John B. Norman pastored the of the Lily of the Valley Baptist Church in the late 1920's. Prior to his coming, Rev. Boston was the pastor. Rev. Boston owned property in the community and lived on the southwest corner of 21st and E. Lovett.

Rev. Norman saw a need to educate Edinburg's black children, so he began teaching them in the church around 1928. Classes were held there until a small, one room school building was constructed behind the church some time later. The school was named Norman, E. W. after the Edwards, West, and Norman families. They provided the school with nearly 25 students over the years.

The school was located on the north side of the church and faced west on 19th Ave. This school served the children until 1938. Lily of the Valley Church, which unlike the school, still stands, faces south and is on the north east corner of E. Van Week and 19th Ave.

According to Gary West's master thesis, "The Weed Was A Flower," written at Pan American University in 1976, Lily of the Valley Church sponsored the school. It also paid all expenses, established objectives, and hired the teacher, Rev. Norman, who served from 1928 until 1931. This information came from Mr. West's grandfather, Vernon West, in a personal interview conducted on November 10, 1974.

On Wednesday, November 5, 1930, Mr. Vernon West arrived in Edinburg with his wife, Maggie, and their five children; Lillie Bell, Haywood, Julian, Edgar, and Milton, who would turn ten Nov. 22. According to Vernon's daughter, Mrs. Lillie Bell Dickens Baker, in a personal interview on June 6, 1998, the trip to Edinburg from Rice, Texas (about 40 miles south of Dallas) took three days and three nights. The travelers had to sleep in the vehicles.

Transportation for the move was provided by a family friend, Mr. Craig, who owned a truck. Those riding in the truck included Mrs. Baker's father, her four brothers and her Uncle, Mitchell West. She reported that the truck had many flat tires on the way so they had to keep stopping to repair them. The women, which included her Aunt Myrtle, Mitchell's wife, rode in a car and were accompanied by Mr. Craig.

Names Of Rio Grande Valley African—American Families

The following list includes names of some of the families who lived in the Edinburg area during the period of time from approximately 1928 to 1961 when the Norman, E. W. and George Washington Carver Schools served African—American children in Edinburg, Texas.

Rev. John B. Norman, pastor of the Lily of the Valley Baptist Church began teaching children in the church around 1928. Classes were held there until a small one room school building was constructed behind the church. The school was named Norman, E. W. after the Edwards, West and Norman families which provided the school with nearly 25 students. The school was located on the north side of the church and faced west on 19th Ave. It is no longer there in 1999. Lily of the Valley Church, which still stands, faces south and is on the north east corner of E. Van Week and 19th.

According to Gary West's master thesis, The Weed Was A Flower, written at Pan American University in 1976, Lily of the Valley Church sponsored the school, paid all the expenses, established objectives, and hired a teacher which was Rev. Norman from 1928 until 1931. This information came from Mr. West's grandfather, Vernon West, in a personal interview conducted on November 10, 1974.

On Wednesday, November 5, 1930, Mr. Vernon West arrived in Edinburg with his wife, Maggie, and their five children—Lillie Bell, Haywood, Julian, Edgar, and Milton who would turn ten Nov. 22. According to Vernon's daughter, Mrs. Lillie Bell Dickens Baker, in a personal interview on June 6, 1998, the trip to Edinburg from Rice (about 40 miles south of Dallas), Texas took three days and three nights. The travelers also had to sleep in the vehicles.

Transportation for the move was provided by a family friend, Mr. Craig, who owned a truck. Those riding in the truck included her father, four brothers and her Uncle, Mitchell West. Mrs. Baker reported that the truck had many flat tires on the way so they had to keep stopping to repair them. The women which included her Aunt Myrtle, Mitchell's wife, rode in a car and were accompanied by Mr. Craig.

Because they had come to the Rio Grande Valley at the request of Rev. Norman, they went right to the Wednesday night church service as soon as they arrived in town and joined the church. Rev. Norman had prepared a home for them on the east side of the Lily of the Valley Church. According to Mrs. Baker, the family had left vegetables in the field and chickens roosting to come to the Valley and start a new life.

Mr. Gary West wrote that the school's "garden" was a cactus grove which made outdoor recreation impossible. However from inside the building, road runner birds were seen zooming by the door rather frequently and occasionally, on fairly cool days, "bell boys" (rattlesnakes) could be seen bathing in the sun.

The Edinburg School District sold old "hand-me-down" textbooks to the church for the Norman, E. W. School students. Their curriculum consisted of reading, writing, and arithmetic.

Mr. Edgar West, Sr. (Vernon West's second youngest son) stated in a personal interview with his nephew, Gary West, on Nov. 3, 1974, that Mrs. Verna Veil Butler followed Rev. Norman as the teacher for the 1931-1932 school year. Then came Miss Ruby Leona Parker who taught for three years from the fall of 1932 until the spring of 1935.

In 1935, Mrs. Melissa Dotson Betts became the last teacher at the Norman, E. W. School. She received her B. A. in elementary education from Texas Southern University in Houston, Texas. Later she earned her M.A. degree. By the spring of 1938, the school had become a credited institution and held its first and last eighth grade graduation. Vernon West's youngest son, Milton, was part of that special class. Unfortunately, no Rio Grande Valley high school would accept African American students. Graduates had to leave their homes and families if they wished to continue their education.

Mr. R. P. Ward who was the superintendent of the Edinburg School District in 1938 met with parents at the Norman, E.W. School to discuss paying the expenses for black students to get high school diplomas in other regions of the state. However, in the end, it was the parents who had to provide the money for their children to attend black high schools elsewhere. Around four years later, about 1942, a Rio Grande Valley black high school was established. It became an extension of McAllen's Booker T. Washington Elementary School. It was located in south McAllen around S. 16th St. and Booker T Street, a few blocks north of present day Expressway 83 and La Plaza Mall. Booker T. Washington High School served all Valley African-American students. They were bussed to McAllen from as far away as Brownsville.

Back in Edinburg, October 11, 1938 marked the dedication for the "Edinburg Colored School". A new building had been constructed in the middle of the block on the south side of E. Lovett St. between 21st and 20th Ave. The school was named for George Washington Carver. Mrs. Betts continued as the only teacher for grades kinder through eighth. She did receive some assistance from time to time from parents like Hattie Mae West.

Mrs. Betts relied on the World War II veterans from the nearby Jacob White American Legion Post #884 to provide the school with playground equipment and other physical education supplies like balls and bats. The men also met with the superintendent to request custodial help for her, but were told that no funds were available for Carver School. Post #884 decided to pay one of the older boys to go school early to get the fire started and to help Mrs. Betts with other cleaning and yard duties that she was expected to do.

Mrs. Betts, with the assistance of parents, conducted arts and crafts classes for the girls and held Girl Scout meetings at school as well. She continued in her same teaching position at Carver School for twenty-two years, until 1961. At that time, the segregated school was closed and she and her students became integrated in with the rest of the Edinburg School District. Mrs. Betts remained with the Edinburg School District until her retirement some years later.

In 1998, her name was submitted along with those of Rev. John B. Norman and Mr. Vernon West for consideration as possible names for the new elementary schools that were being built in the Edinburg Consolidated Independent School District. As of February 1999, the school names had not yet been announced.

CHAPTER I

———◆◆◆———

The Problem And Its Setting

After the Egyptian and Indian, the Greek and Roman, the Teuton and Mongolian, the Negro is a sort of seventh son, born with a veil, and gifted with second-sight in this American world, a world which yields him no true self-consciousness, but only lets him see himself through the revelation of the other world. It is a peculiar sensation, this double-consciousness, this sense of always looking at one's self through the eyes of others, of measuring one's soul by the tape of a world that looks on in amused contempt and pity. One ever feels his twoness, an American a Negro; two souls two thoughts, two unreconcited strivings: two warring ideals in one dark body, whose dogged strength alone keeps it from being torn asunder.

The history of the American Negro is the history of this strife, this longing to attain self-conscious manhood, to merge his double self into a better and truer self. In this merging he wishes neither of

1

the older selves to be lost. He would not Africanize America, for America has too much to teach the world and Africa. He would not bleach his Negro soul in a flood of white Americanism, for he knows that Negro blood has a message for the world. He simply wishes to make it possible for a man to be both a Negro and an American, without being cursed and spit upon by his fellows, without having the doors of opportunity closed roughly in his face.

It was a very slow process covering many years before the black man could open the doors of opportunity. This period has come to be known as the "book learning" stage. The curiosity, born of compulsory ignorance, to know and test the power of the cabalistic letters of the white man, the longing to know. Here at last seemed to have been discovered the mountain path to Canaan, longer than the highway of Emancipation and law, steep and rugged, but leading to heights high enough to overlook life.

This research will deal with a very diminutive section of this "book learning" stage. In various parts of the United States this stage took on diversified forms. However, this paper will be limited to Edinburg, Texas. The learning stage as far as the all American city is concerned took on the form of a one room school house. This is the story about that school. The purpose of this study is to define the role of the black school in the community. Because of the topic it is necessary to unfold many incidents that may offend the reader. Let it be known, that this research will be a factual account of the black school in Edinburg.

Because of the delimitations only a few of the situations and problems can be discussed in any detail. This research will begin with the first black school in Edinburg and end with integration in 1954.

This paper will also analyze why there were no incidents in Edinburg, when the Brown v Board of Education decision was handed down. Thus, begins the pages of black history in the all-American city of Edinburg, Texas.

[Servant of God, Well done;
Thy Glorious Warfare's past;
The battles' fought, the race is won
And thou art crowned at last.]

23rd PSALM

The Lord is my shepherd; I shall not want.

He maketh me to lie down in green pastures: he leadeth me beside the still waters.

He restoreth my soul: he leadeth me in the paths of righteousness for his name's sake.

Yea, though I walk through the valley of the shadow of death, I will fear no evil: for thou art with me, thy rod and they staff they comfort me.

Thou prepares a table before me in the presence of mine enemies: thou anointest my head with oil; my cup runneth over.

Surely goodness and mercy shall follow me all the days of my life: and I will dwell in the house of the Lord forever.

Mrs. Melissa Betts and students of the Carver School

CHAPTER II

History Of The School

Prior to 1928 there was no black school in Edinburg. Rev. J. B. Norman established the first black school in 1928. If there was a father of education in Edinburg, then Rev. Norman is it. At the time the school was established, it was affiliated with Lily Of the Valley Baptist church. The church sponsored the school paying expenses, establishing objectives, and hiring a teacher.[1]

Rev John B. Norman was born in Glenflora, Texas. The date was November 19, 1896, Wharton County. He grew up in Waco, Texas attended Central Texas College and Conroe Normal and Industrial College where he received the Bachelor of Theology Degree. He pastored at Waco, Texas-Marshall Chapel Baptist Church, New Hope Baptist Church of Rice, Texas, Lily of the Valley Baptist church

---

[1]   Vernon West, personal interview, November 10, 1974.

of Edinburg, Texas for twelve years, St. Mary's Baptist church of Houston, Texas for ten years, and in 1953 he was called to Mt. Calvary Baptist Church, Beaumont, Texas, where he served 14 years, one month and two weeks before his death Tuesday, February 28, 1967 at 12:08 P. M. in the Baptist Ministers Union regular weekly meeting. He held positions as moderator of the People' Association, North, Texas and former secretary of the Independent District Association for seven years.[2]

The school under Rev. Norman was named the Edwards, West, and Norman school. The school was located on what is now East Van Week directly behind Lily of the Valley Baptist Church. Rev. Norman served in this capacity from 1928-1931.[3]

During Rev. Norman's initial tutelage there were only two black families in Edinburg. They were the Edwards and the Wests. Rev. Norman decided to use the initials of these two families in the name of the school. The school was called E. W. & Norman. According to their standards these families were normal. They were able to supply the school with close to 25 students.[4]

To say E. W. & Norman was a unique school is to be redundant. However, this school which has come to be known as E. W. & Norman had as its garden a cactus grove. This ruled out any form of recreation at the school. Frequently one could see a road runner

---

[2]   Ibid.
[3]   Ibid.
[4]   Ibid.

zoom by the door. Occasionally on fairy cool days one could see "bell boys" bathing in the sun.[5]

The curriculum at E. W. & Norman consisted of reading, writing and arithmetic. Values were also an essential part of the curriculum. The textbooks used were hand-me-downs from the Edinburg school district. They were sold to the church which sponsored the school. In many cases the information taught had changed and was no longer valid. Even with conditions as rigid as these absentees were small in number. The reward for these pupils was to come some twenty years later, when their sons and daughters would enter fully accredited schools in their district.[6]

E. W. & Norman was the first black school in Edinburg and as the research has pointed out it was a school with several weaknesses. There were strengths in the school also. The advance up the new path was a slow one. Only those who have watched and guided the faltering feet, the misty minds, the dull understandings, of the dark pupils of these schools know how faithfully, how piteously, these people strove to learn. It was weary work. The cold statistician wrote down the inches of progress here and there, noted also where here and there a foot had slipped or someone had fallen. To the students of E. W. & Norman, the horizon was ever dark, the mists were often cold, the Canaan was always dim and far away. If, however, the vistas disclosed as yet no goal, no resting-place, little but flattery and criticism the journey at least gave leisure for reflection and

---

[5]   The term bell boy is a slang phrase used to describe rattle snakes.

[6]   Melissa Dotson Betts, personal interview, October 31, 1974.

self-examination it changed the child on Emancipation to the youth with dawning self-consciousness, self-realization, self-respect. In those dingy forests of his striving, his own soul rose before him, and he saw himself-darkly as through a veil; and yet he saw in himself some faint revelation of his power, of his mission. He began to have a dim feeling that, to attain his place in the world, he must be himself, and not another. For the first time he sought to analyze the burden he bore upon his back, that dead weight of social degradation partially masked behind a half-named Negro problem. He felt his poverty. He felt the weight of his ignorance, not simply of letters, but of life, of business, of the humanities. It was here at E. W. & Norman that the pupils as well as the parents had tasted of the Tree of Life.[7]

Upon Rev. Norman's departure, Mrs. Verna Veil Butler accepted the job. She was a do it yourself teacher at E. W. & Norman. She began her assignment in 1932 and pretty much followed the policies of Rev. Norman. Mrs. Butler only taught for one year.[8]

Miss Ruby Leona Parker succeeded Miss Butler. She taught for three years. Under Miss Parker the school began to take on new form. The curriculum was changed the campus improved. As life would have it Miss Parker stayed only a short time. With this departure the wheels of education in the small black school of E. W. & Norman were altered.

---

[7]   Edgar West Sr., personal interview, November 3, 1974
[8]   Ibid.

CHAPTER III

Melissa Dotson Betts

In 1935 Mrs. Melissa Dotson Betts applied for the job at E. W. & Norman. Her credentials said it all. Mrs. Betts received her B.A. in elementary education at Texas Southern University in Houston, Texas. Later she obtain her M.A. Mrs. Betts specialty was arts and crafts. She loved worked working with her hands.

Mrs. Betts was an unusual person. She had the professional know that never comes to some teachers. She placed values high above everything else in her curriculum. She believed if the Negro cannot stand on his own legs, let him fall. All he deserves is a chance to stand on his own legs! Leave him alone! If you see him on his way to school, let him alone-don't disturb him. If you see him going to the ballot box, let him alone-don't disturb him![9]

---

[9]   Betts, personal interview.

With Mrs. Betts, E. W. & Norman became part of the Edinburg school district. On March 19, 1936 Mrs. Bets was reappointed as teacher of the "Colored school" in a meeting of the school board. Her salary was to be $450 annually. As far as her credentials and her salary go the latter was an uncouth joke.[10]

The following chart is a record of Mrs. Betts salary from 1936 to 1940, Each year the following salaries were approved by the board.[11]

1936	$450
1937	450
1938	495
1939	495
1940	585

This research would like to inject here that in 1940 the tentative salary base in the Edinburg school district was $810 for one year of college training. Add $30 for each additional year of training. $900 for B.A. $30 for each year of experience. Consequently it does not take a mathematical genius to figure out that in 1940 Mrs. Betts legal salary should have been $1020.

Even though Mrs. Betts salary was below par it did not hinder or alter her objectives as a teacher or a person. She continued to serve the community the way she knew best and according to research this

---

[10] Ibid.

[11] Board of Trustees. Edinburg, Texas Vol. 4.

side of her went far past the call of duty. Some of her chores were janitor, lawn boy, coach, nurse, and counselor.[12]

The "Colored School" according to the records, were part of the Edinburg School District. However, in other schools janitors were employed on a yearly base. There was only one school in Edinburg where the teacher and pupils had to cut the grass.[13]

Prior to 1938 there had been no graduation exercises from E. W. & Norman for several reasons. Mainly because prior to this time the school had been an unaccredited institution. In 1938 we have the first group of graduates. They are now ready for high school. There is one problem there is no high school. Will the district pay the expenses for the black students to obtain a high school diploma in other regions of the state! A special meeting was called at E. W. & Norman. Attending this meeting was Superintendent R. P. Ward and the parents of pupils at the school. The decision was no, the parents would have to finance their kids bills.[14]

---

[12] Betts
[13] <u>Ibid</u>.
[14] West, Vernon.

CARVER SCHOOL

Carver Elementary School

CHAPTER IV

George Washington Carver School

On October 11, 1938 a dedication program was held for the naming of the Edinburg Colored School. This marked the beginning of George Washington Carver and the death of E. W. & Norman.[15]

It is fitting that there should be a national memorial to Dr. George Washington Carver. He rose from slavery to become a famous scientist. The list of his achievements as a benefactor of mankind is almost endless . . . . Dr. Carver however will be remembered in the gallery of great Americans not so much for scientific eminence, but rather for quality of the man's spirit. He was, as everyone knows, a Negro. But he triumphed over all obstacles, including that of racial discrimination. Perhaps there is no one in this century whose examples has done more to promote a better understanding between

---

[15]   Langston Hughes, <u>Famous American Negroes</u>, p. 75.

the races. Such greatness partakes of the eternal. Dr. Carver did more than find hidden merits in the peanuts and the sweet potato. He helped to enlarge the American spirit.

E. W. & Norman officially became George Washington Carver on October 11, 1938. It seems strange that the name G. W. Carver is seldom used in the school records. The name that the school board records used interchangeable is Colored School. This is not to say what is right or wrong. It would seem that if a school would go through so much trouble to have a dedication service, the least the board could do is acknowledge the name.

Another interesting fact is that the Colored school was frequently referred to, as the rural school. This paper does not question the validity of such classification. The issue is not the amount of students attending the school, but the rural objectives infringe upon the school. Another interesting thing about Carver school is how did the rural students get to school?

The rural students attending Carver school were limited to one family, who lived about six miles from the school. This family because of racial prejudices had to walk to school. This surely was a decretory issue. Research shows that the family that lived next door was able to use the bus. Through a letter submitted to the Texas Educational Agency by superintendent, R.P. Ward integration on buses were to precede integration in schools of Edinburg by fifteen years.[16]

---

[16]   Betts.

Edinburg was quite different from other large cities, even though the schools were segregated many forms of integration were prevalent. Most of them under the direction of Phil Jordan. For quite a while recreational activities were limited to softball at Carver. With the coming of Mr. Jordan many other revenues of recreation were open. During the winter months, every Monday night students from Carver school were taken to the skating rink in McAllen. During the summer months every other Tuesday was a swimming day. The students were bussed to Delta Lake. The bus driver was none other than Phil Jordan. He coached the school as well giving lessons in football and baseball. When organized little League started in Edinburg, Phil Jordan was instrumental in opening the doors for blacks. In field day events, which was the city track meet. George Washington Carver competed with all the schools in the Edinburg district.[17]

What about the girls? Members of a girl organization known as the sub debs would periodically visit the school from Edinburg High. They would instruct the girls in twirling and various activities. The girls were also active in the Girl Scouts.They were allowed to enter various established camps throughout the valley. The veil of racial prejudices slowly begins to unfold.[18]

There is in America today a generation of white youth that is truly worthy of a black man's respect, and this is a rare event in the foul annals of American history. From the beginning of the contact between blacks and whites, there has been little reason for a black

---

[17]   Phil Jordan, personal interview, November 1, 1974.

[18]   Betts.

man to respect a white, with such exceptions as John Brown and other lesser known. Respect controls itself and it can neither be given nor withheld when it is due.[19]

There were also many activities that were run by Mrs. Betts. The 31st of October was Halloween night at Carver school. This was a night the pupils look forward to. On this night everyone would wear costumes. Prizes were given to the best costumes. Also there was the bobbing of apples. Another big day was Christmas Eve. On this day the school play was run off, and there was the exchanging of gifts. Speeches were recited and carols were sung.[20]

The atmosphere at Carver was a gay one. You could never tell by the students that they were lowering the standards of efficiency, that their training was inferior, that the school was inferior. These scars were to perpetuate later in life. Like when applying for a job. However, the students at Carver had been to the mountain top, their only consolation was the dream that their children would make it to the other side.[21]

Nineteen fifty four is held to be a crucial turning point in the history of the Afro American-for the United States as a while-the year segregation was outlawed by the United States Supreme Court in the Brown V Board of Education decision. 1954 was also a crucial year for George Washington Carver School, because the

---

[19]   This research advocates this.

[20]

[21]   Betts.

birth of integration was the death of segregation. In 1954 George Washington Carver School became a thing of the past. A story in the pages of history that would always exist in the minds of the black students. The time of shame is over. The burden of ignorance has been transferred on the Negroes back.

CHAPTER V

Findings And Implications

In a final analysis we can see the black school in Edinburg played a vital role in the community. Through George Washington Carver the students were able to attain self-conscious manhood, to merge his double self into a better and truer self. This does not mean that the school did not also hinder him, for it did. Not only did one teacher teach six different grades, but had to get up early during the winter months and start the fire. This one teacher was janitor and all.

The questions of the future are the number one priority in this research. The incidents and analogies used in this paper were not used for brooding purposes, but to inform the reader of the various circumstances that black schools have encountered. The questions of the future is not to cry over the wrong of the past and the difficulties of the present. The sins of the fathers are visited upon the heads of the children—but only if the children continue in the evil deeds of the parents.

Blacks in the world, Afro-Americans included, do not seek revenge for their suffering. They seek the same things other people want: an end to war and exploitation. The price of hating other human beings is loving oneself less.

As this paper has pointed out George Washington Carver and E.W. & Norman both served a purpose. In the pages of their history there are the names of some respectable white men alone with the black ones. According to research integration was quite an occurrence because of some commendable moves made by people of the community. Because of men like Phil Jordan integration in Edinburg was a delayed occurrence.

As to the question of the usefulness of the school, it can be summarized in one phrase. "The Weed Was a Flower". The black schools in Edinburg truly served a purpose, as did all the schools of this caliber. These small inferior institutions caused incidents that were vital to both histories; black as well as white.

Black schools helped the black man to find himself. He found his identity through the school. This identity was and is the most essential thing for man, race, or nation. With the discovery of identity one can draw analogies about his place or position in the world. Identity was not the objectives of these schools, and one should note that this identity was the result of many years of struggle. It was not an overnight occurrence.

This is not to say that all blacks have self-identity, for they don't. Black inferior schools were wonderful if you compared them with other black schools.

"The darkest hour is just before the dawn". Surely, at E.W. & Norman and G.W. Carver there must have been some dark years, but now we can look back on those days with admiration for the Weed was a flower.

BIBLIOGRAPHY

Primary Sources
<u>Manuscripts</u>

Board of Trustees, vol. IV Edinburg Consolidated Independent School District.

Betts, Melissa, personal interview, October 31, 1974.

Jordan, Phil, personal interview, November 1, 1974.

West, Edgar, personal interview, November 3, 1974.

West, Hattie, personal interview, November 5, 1974.

West, Edgar, personal interview, November 3, 1974.

Secondary Sources
<u>Newspapers</u>

"Rev. White Reviews Negro School Situation in Edinburg", The <u>Daily Review</u>, September 16, 1950.

DuBois, W.E. <u>The Souls of Black Folk</u>, New York, Fawcett Publication Incorporation.

Hughes, Langston, <u>Famous American Negroes</u>, New York, Dodd, Mead & Company 1954.

Norman, J.B., Obituary, Beaumont, Texas 1964.

www.ingramcontent.com/pod-product-compliance
Lightning Source LLC
Chambersburg PA
CBHW061229280526
45784CB00006B/2693